GRASSLAND

APRIL PULLEY SAYRE

TWENTY-FIRST CENTURY BOOKS

A Division of Henry Holt and Company
• New York •

To Patti, Ken, and Jeff, for our coreopsis days
and for my excellent editors, Virginia Ann Koeth and Patricia Culleton.
~ A.P.S. ~

ACKNOWLEDGMENT

A special thanks to Dr. Hal Nagel of the University of Nebraska, who
reviewed parts of this manuscript

Twenty–First Century Books
A Division of Henry Holt and Company, Inc.
115 West 18th Street
New York, NY 10011

Library of Congress Cataloging–in–Publication Data
Sayre, April Pulley.
Grassland / April Pulley Sayre. —1st ed.
p. cm. — (Exploring earth's biomes)
Includes index.
1. Grassland ecology—Juvenile literature. 2. Grasslands—Juvenile
literature. 3. Prairie ecology—North America—Juvenile literature. 4.
Prairies—North America—Juvenile literature. [1. Grasslands. 2.
Grassland ecology. 3. Ecology.] I. Title. II. Series: Sayre, April Pulley.
Exploring earth's biomes.
QH541.5.P7S28 1994   574.5'2643—dc20
                                              94–19389

ISBN 0–8050–2827–7
First Edition—1994

Printed in the United States of America
All first editions are printed on acid–free paper ∞.
10 9 8 7 6 5 4 3 2

PHOTO CREDITS
p. 8: Tom Bean; p. 25: Mark Burnett/Photo Researchers, Inc.; p. 27: John
Eastcott/Yva Momatiuk/The Image Works; p. 31: Alan G. Nelson/Earth
Scenes; p. 38: Betty Derig/Photo Researchers, Inc.; p. 40: J. R. Simon/Photo
Researchers, Inc.; p. 42: Tom McHugh/Photo Researchers, Inc.; p. 46: Bill
Sallaz/Gamma Liaison; p. 52: Martin Bond/Science Photo Library/Photo
Researchers, Inc.

CONTENTS

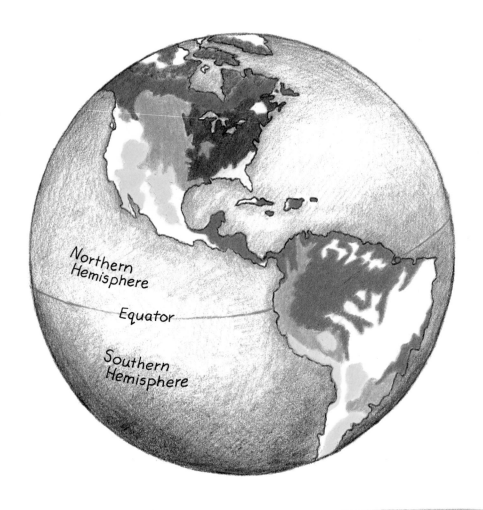

Northern
Hemisphere

Equator

Southern
Hemisphere

rain forest
grassland
desert
temperate deciduous forest
taiga
tundra

INTRODUCTION

Take a look at the earth as a whole and you'll see its surface can be divided into living communities called biomes. Desert, rain forest, tundra, taiga, temperate deciduous forest, grassland, and polar desert are some of the main terrestrial biomes—biomes on land. Each biome has particular kinds of plants and animals living in it. Scientists also identify other biomes not mentioned here, including aquatic biomes—biomes of lakes, streams, and the sea.

When their boundaries are drawn on a globe, terrestrial biomes look like horizontal bands stacked up from Pole to Pole. Starting from the equator and moving outward toward the Poles, you'll find rain forests, grasslands, deserts, and grasslands once again. Then things change a little. The next biomes we think of—temperate deciduous forests, taiga, and tundra—exist only in the Northern Hemisphere. Why is this true? Well, if you look in the Southern Hemisphere, you'll see there's very little land in the regions where these biomes would supposedly lie. There's simply nowhere for these biomes to exist! Conditions on small pieces of land—islands and peninsulas—that lie in these areas are greatly affected by sea conditions and are very different from those on continents.

But why do biomes generally develop in these bands? The answer lies in the earth's climate and geology. Climate is affected by the angle at which sunlight hits the earth. At the equator, sunlight passes through the atmosphere and hits the earth straight on, giving it its full energy. At the Poles, sunlight must pass through more atmosphere and it hits the earth at an angle, with less energy per square foot. Other factors also influence where biomes lie: the bands of rising and falling air that circulate around the planet; the complex weather systems created by jutting mountains, deep valleys, and cold currents; the glaciers that have scoured the lands in years past; and the activities of humans. These make biome boundaries less regular than the simplified bands described above.

1
THE GRASSLAND BIOME

Imagine a place where the land stretches out and the sky seems wide, where wind whips the grass into waves, where grazing animals roam in great herds, and there are so few trees that you can see for many miles. This is grassland.

In South Africa, it's called veld; in Eurasia, it's steppe. In Australia, it's called rangeland; in South America, pampa; and in North America, prairie. Yet despite these regional names, grasslands worldwide share many features. They're grassy, windy, and dry, but not so dry they become desert. Most have grazing and browsing animals: pronghorn antelope and bison in North America; kangaroos in Australia; llamas in South America; and zebras, giraffes, and dozens of other species in Africa. Perhaps most noticeable of all, grasslands around the world support very few trees.

Though short on trees, grasslands nevertheless contain much more than grass. Hundreds of wildflower species such as sunflowers, coneflowers, bee balms, shooting stars, and lilies create a colorful, seasonal bloom in North America's prairies. Cacti and scattered trees and shrubs add variety to the scene, while along streams and wetlands, water-loving plants and animals thrive.

Over the face of the grasslands, some of the world's most riveting predator–prey dramas are played out. In Africa, lions gather around a kill, and a cheetah—the world's fastest land animal—sprints to bring down an

Severe weather, including dramatic lightning, often occurs over the Great Plains.

antelope. While in North America, wolves move in to kill a bison many times their own size.

Like desert or tundra, grassland is a biome—a geographic area that has a certain kind of climate and a certain community of plants and animals. About a quarter of earth's land is grassland. Geographically, this biome occurs on every continent except Antarctica. Grasslands exist on either side of the two desert belts that circle the earth. Tropical grasslands—those grasslands closest to the equator—are hot year-round. While temperate grasslands—those grasslands farther from the equator—experience both hot summers and harsh winters.

In this book we'll focus on temperate grasslands, specifically North America's prairies. We'll explore their sights, sounds, and smells, from flowers blooming, prairie dogs kissing, and prairie chickens dancing to the grander spectacles—the powerful hailstorms, dust storms, raging fires, and strong tornadoes that plague these lands.

GRASSLAND AT A GLANCE

TYPES

There are two main types of grasslands:

- **Tropical grasslands** These grasslands are located near the equator, between the Tropic of Cancer and the Tropic of Capricorn. Often called savanna, these grasslands are hot year-round. Though dry overall, they do experience wet seasons of torrential rain.
- **Temperate grasslands** Located in the temperate region, north of the Tropic of Cancer, or south of the Tropic of Capricorn, these grasslands have hot summers and cold winters.

Most of this book refers to temperate grasslands only.

TEMPERATURES

- Air temperatures are very hot in summer, up to 113°F (45°C); yet they are very cold in winter, down to -49°F (-45°C).
- Average yearly temperature varies, from 39°F to 46°F (4°C to 8°C) in the northern mixed-grass prairie to 59°F (15°C) in the desert grassland.

WEATHER

- Windy.
- Generally dry climate, with periodic droughts for weeks, months, or years.
- Temperate grasslands in North America average 8 to 39 inches (20 to 100 centimeters) of precipitation per year. Evaporation rates can be high, so little of the rain soaks into the soil.

SOIL

- Ranging from deep black to light brown, prairie soils vary between slightly acid to slightly alkaline, and are generally rich in organic matter—decayed animals and plants.

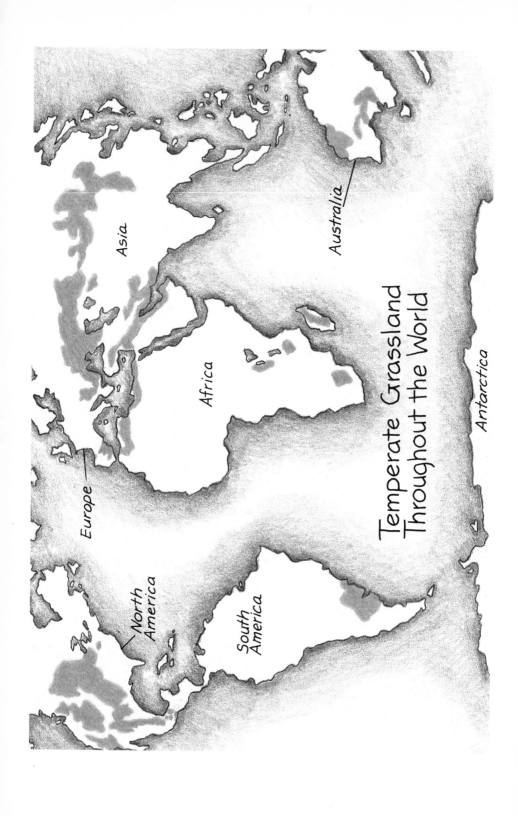

Temperate Grassland
Throughout the World

Asia

Europe

Africa

Australia

North
America

South
America

Antarctica

- Soil in wetter grassland regions, such as the tallgrass prairie, is considered among the world's best for farming.

PLANTS
- Most grasslands have fewer than one tree per acre, although tropical savannas may have more.
- Grasslands support grasses, forbs (plants, other than grasses, that lack woody stems), scattered cacti, shrubs, and trees.
- Many grassland plants are deep-rooted and adapted to drought, fire, and grazing.

ANIMALS
- Animal species diversity—the number of different kinds of animals—is moderate.
- Grazing animals are common. Burrowing animals such as prairie dogs, gophers, and ground squirrels are also numerous.
- Insects are abundant.

2
GRASSLAND IN NORTH AMERICA

To the early European-American settlers who crossed them, North America's grasslands seemed like an ocean of grass. In places, grass grew tall enough to hide a horse. Some settlers, accustomed to forests, felt exposed and uncomfortable on the expanses of grass, with little shelter, and seemingly endless open space. Other travelers fell in love with the land's beauty: the colorful flowers that grew among the grasses, and the strange, bright quality of light that shone down upon the prairie.

Whether they hated or loved the prairie, enough people remained so that within 100 years what had once been a land of millions of buffalo, hunted by small tribes of nomadic Native Americans, became a settled land, a planted land, a grazed land. In the United States, grassland historically covered 914 million acres (366 million hectares), a larger area than any other terrestrial biome. These grasslands stretched from what is today Edmonton, in Alberta, Canada, almost to Mexico City, Mexico, and covered areas in America as far west as California and as far east as Indiana and Ohio.

Ecologists divide North American grassland into six major regions. Three of these lie at the heart of the continent. The short-grass prairie begins at the foot of the Rocky Mountains and stretches eastward. There it meets the

Short-grass Prairie

Inter-mountain Grassland

Mixed-grass Prairie

Canada

United States

Tallgrass Prairie

Temperate Grassland in North America

California Grassland

Desert Grassland

Mexico

mixed-grass prairie, which clothes the Great Plains of Canada and the United States. Farthest east, the tallgrass prairie extends to the ragged edge of the temperate deciduous forest in Indiana and Ohio. North America's three other major grassland regions are the intermountain grassland in the northwestern United States, the desert grassland in the southwestern United States, and the central valley grassland in California. Each of the six major grassland regions is described below. Not described here are countless smaller pockets of grassland that lie on mountains, near coasts, and in other portions of North America.

SHORT-GRASS PRAIRIE

As its name indicates, the short-grass prairie has short grass, less than 2 feet (61 centimeters) tall. Blue grama and buffalo grass are the dominant species. The westernmost of the three central prairies, the short-grass prairie blankets a

200-mile- (323-kilometer-) wide belt at the foot of the Rockies. What little precipitation this area does receive—in places only 10 inches (25 centimeters) or so each year—comes mostly as rain in summer. Today grazing is common on this dry land, where soils are often shallow and unsuitable for farming without irrigation.

MIXED-GRASS PRAIRIE

Although it covers more area than any other North American grassland region, this prairie is nonetheless an "in-between" land. It supports a mixture of grasses from short-grass and tallgrass prairies, as well as species of its own. Wetter than short-grass prairie, yet drier than tallgrass prairie, it receives 14 to 23 inches (36 to 58 centimeters) of precipitation per year, primarily as summertime rain. Most of its grasses are of medium height, between 2 and 4 feet (61 and 122 centimeters). Common species include little bluestem, western wheatgrass, side-oats grama, needlegrass, June grass, three awns, and various sedges.

TALL GRASS PRAIRIE

This prairie supports tall grasses that grow to over 5 feet (1½ meters) high. Big bluestem, little bluestem, Indian grass, and switchgrass are the most common grass species. This lush growth is due to the relatively plentiful precipitation the area receives—25 to 39 inches (64 to 99 centimeters) per year, which arrives mostly as rain in summer. Today almost all the tallgrass prairie has been converted to farmland. The largest remaining expanse is in the Flint Hills region of Kansas.

DESERT GRASSLAND

Located at the edges of the Sonora and Chihuahuan deserts, this grassland grows on high plateaus. Common plant species include grasses such as Indian ricegrass and black grama. Though mostly dry, desert grassland does experience summer rains and winter rains and snow, totalling 11 to 17 inches (28 to 43 centimeters) of precipitation each year. Over the last 100 years, much of this grassland has changed, as grasses have disappeared, and shrubs such as mesquite and creosote bush have taken over the land. Scientists aren't sure why this change has occurred, but it may be caused by cattle overgrazing, climate change, or the absence of fire.

CALIFORNIA GRASSLAND
This grassland covers parts of the San Joaquin valley, Sacramento valley, and Los Angeles basin in California. Originally, grasses such as wild rye, June grass, needlegrass, three awn, and deer grass dominated the scene. But because of overgrazing and competition with introduced plant species from farm fields and human habitation, these native plants are not as common today. However, spring still brings a breathtaking bloom of native poppies, lupine, coreopsis, and buttercups to this region.

INTERMOUNTAIN GRASSLAND
This grassland spreads across parts of Wyoming, eastern Washington State, eastern Oregon, southwestern Idaho, and western Montana, up into southwestern Canada. Bluebunch wheatgrass and sagebrush are common. The intermountain grassland gets most of its precipitation in winter. In areas ungrazed by cattle, grasses can grow lush. However, many areas are overgrazed by cattle, and as a result have only short, sparse grasses and an abundance of shrubs.

3
GRASSLAND WEATHER, CLIMATE, AND GEOLOGY

In between the world's deserts and forests lie its grasslands. Too dry for forest, but wet enough for grass to grow, these "in-between" lands nevertheless have their own distinctive weather, climate, and geology.

A LAND OF EXTREMES
Grassland weather is not for the faint of heart. North American prairie dwellers may swelter in summer temperatures as high as 113°F (45°C) yet freeze in winter temperatures that can dip to -49°F (-45°C). Of course, these are the extremes. The weather you'll experience on a visit to North America's prairie is likely to be milder, depending on which grassland you visit and the time of year.

Windy and Dry   One of the great challenges of grassland living, for animals and plants alike, is dryness. Rainfall in North America's prairies ranges from low to moderate. But dry winds and hot sun rapidly evaporate rainwater off the dead stalks and leaves that cover the ground. As a result, much of the rain that falls never soaks into the soil. In addition, droughts—periods when there is little or no rain—can occur every few decades.

Prairies do have their wet spots. Wetlands may form where water draining off other land collects, or where snowdrifts build up and then melt.

Stormy Weather   Despite their generally dry weather, temperate grasslands still receive precipitation in the form of rain and snow. Severe, violent weather, created by the clashing of air masses from the Pacific, Arctic, and Gulf Coast can produce heavy rains, high winds, lightning, tornadoes, blizzards, and even golf-ball-sized hail. Winter on the plains is usually bitterly cold and dry. High winds can scour the snow off the land, heaping it into drifts.

A Wide Range   Weather and climatic factors vary across North America's grassland regions. On average, North America's tallgrass prairie receives 39 inches (100 centimeters) of precipitation annually. Yet desert grasslands, intermountain grasslands, and the central valley grasslands get much less, about 8 to 12 inches (20 to 30 centimeters) per year. Among North America's central prairies, precipitation decreases from east to west. The tallgrass prairie gets 39 inches (100 centimeters) of precipitation per year, while the mixed-grass prairie receives 20 inches (50 centimeters), and the short-grass prairie receives 8 inches (20 centimeters). Also, in each grassland, precipitation peaks at certain times of year, according to the local climate.

RICH SOILS

Dark in color, rich in organic matter, and often several feet deep, the tallgrass prairie's topsoil is a farmer's dream. This soil, called *mollisol*, meaning "soft soil," is among the best farming soils in the world. That's one reason so much of the tallgrass prairie has been plowed under for growing crops. Much of the soil's richness comes from its plants, whose fibrous roots decay, giving the soil its dark color.

Wet to Dry   Soil characteristics vary from region to region. As you travel west across North America's grasslands, to the drier prairies, you'll find the topsoil becomes progressively shallower, lighter in color, and less rich in organic matter. In these drier grasslands, including the short-grass prairie, desert grassland, intermountain grassland, and California grassland, a lime layer not far below the soil surface can prevent water and roots from penetrating deeply. In these areas, growing conditions are more difficult than in the tallgrass prairie. These drier grasslands are often used for grazing cattle instead of growing crops.

WHAT'S IN SOIL?

Soil is much more than bits of rock and decayed plants and animals. Soil is partly alive, full of tiny creatures that are important in the cycling of nutrients within the soil. Without these organisms, many plants cannot grow. To discover some of the organisms that live in soil, construct a Berlese funnel.

You'll need:
- Sharp knife
- Plastic gallon-size milk jug with lid or 2-liter soda bottle with cap
- Small jar
- String
- Ring stand or some other stand to hold the setup
- Some long-stemmed grass
- Several cups of soil
- Desk lamp
- Hand lens (magnifying glass)
- Tray or dish

1. Ask an adult to help you use the knife to cut the bottom off the milk jug or soda bottle.
2. Set up the lamp, ring stand, jar, and bottle or jug as shown in the illustration. The string will help hold the bottle steady as it rests on the stand.
3. Place some long-stemmed grass in the bottom of the bottle,

plastic bottle with lid

ring stand

soil sample

grass

Cut off bottom.

covering the inside of the lid. This will help prevent soil from falling out during the experiment. However, you shouldn't put so much grass that it prevents organisms from crawling through.

4. Collect a soil sample, down to about 7 inches (18 centimeters) deep, from land nearby. (Ask for permission if needed!) Several cups of soil should do for a good sample.

5. Pour your soil sample into the bottle. Carefully remove the bottle lid.

6. Turn on the lamp. The heat of the lamp will dry the soil surface, driving the soil organisms downward to the moister soil. Eventually, they will crawl out the bottom and fall into the collecting jar. How long it takes for this to happen depends on the heat of the lamp, the moisture in the soil, and the creatures contained in the soil. Using your Berlese funnel, you may find a variety of organisms: springtails, mites, beetles, fly larvae, and others.

7. Once you have collected a sufficient number of soil organisms, remove the jar and examine the organisms on a tray or dish, using a hand lens to examine what you find.

8. When you have finished examining the organisms, return them, and the soil from the bottle, to the place where they were collected.

EARTH ALERT: THE DIRT ON DIRT

Topsoil may not sound like the world's most exciting topic of conversation, but it's of vital importance. Your life, and the lives of just about everyone else in the world, depends upon good-quality topsoil—the soil near the ground's surface, the soil plants' roots penetrate. Unfortunately, very little of the earth's soil is good for farming. What good topsoil there is, if improperly treated, can become salty, or nutrient poor, or too dry for farming. It can even blow away on a dry, windy day.

Green Acres Lost   At one time, the prairie plants' thick, intertwined roots kept the prairie soils intact and contributed to their fertility. But now much of that soil is plowed for farming and churned up by cattle's hooves. In many places this soil disturbance has led to erosion, with soil blowing away and washing into streams and rivers at an alarming rate. That's tragic, considering the dark, thick, rich prairie topsoil is among the continent's best. It can take nature 7,000 years to form an 8-inch (20-centimeter) layer of topsoil. Yet that same 8-inch layer can be destroyed by bad farming practices in only 40 years! Soil conservation techniques, however, can make that soil last for 2,000 or more years of farming. Today some farmers are using these techniques to improve their harvest, and ensure healthy soil for the future.

TOPOGRAPHY

Most grassland occurs on relatively flat land, or low-rolling hills; but landforms vary from region to region. For instance, North America's desert grassland lies on high-altitude plateaus. The intermountain grassland occurs literally in between mountains. The short-grass, mixed-grass, and tallgrass prairies cover a large plain that slopes gently from the Rocky Mountains to the Mississippi River. In the northern plains, thousands of water-filled depressions called prairie potholes make the land, when viewed from above, look a little like Swiss cheese.

GRASSLANDS ON THE MOVE

There was a time, 65 million years ago, when forests and an inland sea existed where North American grasslands are today. But then, something dramatic happened: the Laramide Revolution. The earth buckled, and wrinkled, and the Sierra Nevadas, Sierra Madres, and Rocky Mountains were formed. (The Appalachian Mountains, which are much older, already existed.) Once formed, these relatively new mountains changed the climate of the continent forever.

Mountainous Barriers   Pacific winds, which once blew moist air across most of the continent, now encountered the high mountain peaks. As the air was forced up over the mountains, it cooled, dropping much of its moisture. By the time the air reached the other side of the mountains, the water had been wrung out of it. Wind now blew dry over the land between the Rockies and the Appalachians. So these lands became too dry for forest, and the forests died out. Grassland developed.

Changing Climate   Over the millions of years since the Laramide Revolution, the borders of grassland and forest have shifted back and forth. For instance, at times, in the past, glacial ice has covered more than half of what is now grassland. At those times, neither forest nor grassland grew on the land that was buried deep beneath the ice, which was a mile thick in some places. Less drastic changes over thousands of years have caused the climate to become drier and grasslands to spread widely. (At one time, prairie plants grew as far east as Pennsylvania!) At other times, cool, moist air from the Gulf of Mexico has moved farther north and west, creating conditions that changed grassland to for-

21

est. Even in modern times, the range of grassland types can shift from decade to decade and from year to year. During dry years, such as the Dust Bowl years of the 1930s, short-grass prairie moves farther east, while in wetter years tall-grass and mixed-grass prairies shift westward.

• DUST BOWL DAYS •

Just think of what it would be like waking up one morning to find a cloud of dirt has covered half your house, has buried the tractor in the yard, and has choked the crops where they grew in your fields. Your own mouth, nose, and lungs are full of the dust. The air is filled with dirt everywhere, even inside the house. There is no escaping it. That is what it was like on some American farms during the Dust Bowl of the 1930s.

One of the worst environmental disasters in United States history, the Dust Bowl occurred after several years of severe drought, when the grass and crops growing on the Great Plains died. The soil dried out, and windstorms blew great clouds of soil all the way from the prairies to New York City. In just one storm, an estimated 12 million tons (11 mil-lion metric tons) of dust were dumped on Chicago. Carried by wind, prairie soil even landed on ships out in the Atlantic Ocean! This soil came from the "dust bowl"—a grassland area of Texas, New Mexico, Colorado, Kansas, and Oklahoma, where the worst drought and dust storms hit. Other prairie areas, extending north through the Dakotas and Montana into Canada, were also affected.

In these lands, farms failed and people were thrown into poverty. Dust blew into drifts 25 feet (7.6 meters) high, burying farm machinery. Many people died of respiratory diseases. Bits of dirt rubbing together in the air caused a buildup of static electricity so severe that some automobile ignitions failed. And the storms continued into the 1940s. ⟶

What caused the Dust Bowl? Both climatic factors and people's actions. Drought is a natural part of grassland life, occurring every 20 to 22 years in some parts of the North American grassland. Yet people's actions intensified the effects of the drought. For thousands of years, the soils of North America's grassland had been held relatively intact by the strong roots of prairie plants. But widespread farming turned up the dirt, drying it out. Yearly plowing broke the prairie plants' roots, making it easier for the soil to dry out and blow away. And the crops resown on the soils were usually plants such as wheat or corn, which did not produce widespread root growth to hold the soil in place.

Because of the tragedy of the Dust Bowl, in 1936 the United States government established the Soil Conservation Service to help people learn how to reduce soil erosion. Thousands of trees were planted on the prairie as windbreaks. Terraces were built to distribute rainwater. Hundreds of new wells were dug to draw water from underground. Farmers began plowing along the contours of the land, instead of in straight rows. This helped water soak into the soil.

In the years since the Dust Bowl of the 1930s, droughts and dust storms have continued to plague North America's farms. In the 1950s and 1970s, huge dust storms carried away acres of fertile soil. The threat of such ecological disaster remains today. In the past 20 years, many farmers have stopped carrying out the conservation practices begun after the Dust Bowl. As a result, the Soil Conservation Service and concerned farmers and environmentalists are working together to encourage other farmers to use soil conservation methods, both old and new. No one wants to see another Dust Bowl.

4
GRASSLAND PLANTS

Grass is among the hardiest plants on earth. Bison, cows, and other grazers eat its leaves, but still, it grows back. Fire may burn it down to the ground, but still it thrives in the charred black soil. Long droughts may kill much of it off, but still grass returns, sprouting from seed or rising from special stems tucked deep underground. And each spring, after its dead stalks have been beaten down by ice, snow, and wind during the cold winter, grass rises again from food stored in its extensive roots. Although many other kinds of plants also live in grasslands, the story of this biome begins with grass—a truly remarkable plant.

GRASSES: KEYS TO THEIR SUCCESS

Grasses—the 7,500 species belonging to the Gramineae family—grow in a variety of habitats, from alpine meadows to desert grasslands to freshwater marshes. Adaptations have made this plant family successful in various grassland regions.

Dangerous Dryness Living in a dry climate, with long, hot summers and strong winds, grassland plants run the risk of drying out. Fortunately, prairie grasses, with their needlelike shape, expose very little surface area to the hot sun and drying wind. For even better protection, some grasses slow down during the heat of summer, decreasing their respiratory rate so they take in less hot, dry air and release less water to the environment. Grasses such as bluestem go even a step further. When they begin to dry out, their leaves fold up like a tube. This helps to prevent moisture from escaping.

Mowable Meristems   Most plant types grow from their tips. Not so with grasses. They grow upward from their base. Because a grass plant's meristem—the spot where cells multiply and growth originates—is located near the base, it is less likely to be damaged by nibbling animals or lawn mowers. This feature helps grasses survive grazing and enables homeowners to mow their lawn without killing it. This sort of damage could be devastating to other kinds of plants, which need to grow whole new branches or stems if their tips are removed.

Tip of the Rootberg   There's more to a prairie grass than what you see at first. That's because as much as 70 percent of a prairie grass's tissue lies underground. Its extraordinary root system can have long roots that tap water deep in

Grass grows upward from its base, enabling it to survive mowing.

the soil, or thick root mats that soak up water from a widespread area. Food stored in these roots helps grass regrow quickly after a cold winter, or a fire. Long, strong roots anchor the grass firmly, so nibbling grazers don't pull up the whole plant. And by absorbing soil moisture and taking up space, grasses' roots can prevent other plants from becoming established. Just how extensive are these root systems? One single grass may have 2 or 3 miles (3.2 or 4.8 kilometers) of roots and root hairs!

Sods, Clumps, and Clones   In moist grasslands, some grasses form thick carpets of intertwined roots called sod. Because sod is so thickly intertwined, European-American settlers cut it into blocks and used it to build houses! Sod is formed when a plant sends out above ground stems, called stolons, or belowground stems, called rhizomes. These stolons and rhizomes eventually root and form a series of connected plants that are tightly packed together. These plants are clones, meaning they are genetically identical to the original plant. In drier prairies, grasses form widely spaced plant clumps instead of closely packed sod.

Growing Types   Both grasses that form sod and those that form clumps are perennials, meaning they survive from year to year. But some prairie grasses sprout, grow, produce seeds, and die, all in one year. These grasses are called annuals. In order to spread, annuals must rely entirely on seeds, whereas perennials can also form clones. Annual grasses come in two main types: cool-season annuals and warm-season annuals. Cool-season annuals sprout in fall and do most of their growing in springtime. Warm-season annuals sprout in spring and do most of their growing in late spring and summer.

Seeds of Success   Grasses are well equipped for colonizing new areas. Grasses—especially annuals—tend to pro-

This replica of a prairie pioneer's sod house shows the sort of snug home that can be made from thick root mats of prairie grasses.

duce seeds in large amounts. Many grasses produce seeds with outer shells called pericarps that keep seeds fresh and viable for long periods of time. This feature allows the seeds to sprout after lying dormant in the soil for many years. These very same characteristics make grasses a good food crop, because their seeds—such as rice grains and wheat grains—are produced in quantity, and can be stored for a long time.

Ouch! Hitchhikers!   If you've ever walked through a field, you've probably experienced seed dispersal firsthand. Your pants, socks, and shoes can end up covered with hitchhiking seeds. Some grass seeds work like Velcro, hooking onto animal fur in order to travel. Other seeds have a nastier

27

habit. Their tiny, barbed bristles screw their way into an animal's fur and skin, sometimes causing painful sores. In response to changes in temperature and humidity, the barbs twist and untwist. Eventually, if conditions change, the seeds may drop off the animal. Their "twisting" adaptation may then allow the seed to twist down into the soil.

Jet Setters   Hitchhiking isn't the only way grass seeds travel. Wind can work just as well. Light, fluffy grass seeds can travel far, especially on the windy days common on prairies. The seeds of one grass were gathered by a research plane traveling at an altitude of 4,000 feet (1,200 meters)!

Anti-grazing Devices   At the edge of prairie wetlands, tough, wiry sloughgrass grows 9 feet (2.7 meters) tall. Fast growing, and abundant, this grass might seem like a good meal for a grazer. But when mature this grass, nicknamed "ripgut," has an effective defense: stiff, serrated, razorlike leaves. These leaves can cut an animal's mouth or a humans' hands. However, by wearing gloves and working carefully, many early prairie farmers harvested this grass, using its tough stalks and leaves for roof thatching, or twisting it into stiff rods to burn like wood. Sloughgrass isn't the only prairie plant with effective defenses. Most grasses contain lots of silica, a sandy, abrasive element that wears away grazing animals' teeth. Other plants contain hard-to-digest lignin or poisonous phenols. All these adaptations help plants fend off the host of animals trying to eat them.

OTHER PRAIRIE PLANTS:
FORBS, SEDGES, CACTI, AND SHRUBS

Turkscap lily, prairie blazing star, western sunflower, purple coneflower, little rattlepod, silky aster, butterfly weed, horsemint, evening primrose, showy goldenrod, spiderwort, compass plant: prairie plant names only hint at the bright and varied parade of flowers that bloom in grasslands each year. All the plants listed above are forbs. *Forb* is the name given to non-grass, broadleafed plants that don't have woody stems as trees and shrubs do.

Tough but Beautiful Like grasses, prairie forbs are adapted for surviving tough prairie conditions. To seek water in the soil, many forbs have deep, branched taproots, reaching as much as 20 feet (6 meters) below the ground's surface. Many forbs are long-lived perennials, surviving 20 or even 50 years. To conserve water, their leaves, while broader than the leaves of grasses, tend to be smaller than those of plants in more humid biomes. The leaves may also have leathery or hairy coverings. Unlike grasses, which have tiny, often dull-colored flowers, forbs are the showy plants of the prairie scene. Each spring and summer, the blooming of the forbs in the prairie is one of the greatest spectacles on earth.

Other Inhabitants Colorful forbs aren't the only plants you'll find amid the grasses. Prickly pear cacti, armed with thick, water-storing leaves, thrive in dry prairies. Sedges and rushes, which are much like grasses, are common in grassland, too. And shrubs, many of which have water-conserving leaves that are light colored, wax coated, and hairy, also grow well in some grasslands. Mesquite and creosote bush—two dryland shrubs—are common in desert grassland in the southwestern United States and northern Mexico. In fact, most grasslands have more species of non-grasses than grasses! However, the amount of grass typically outweighs the amount of plant matter produced by other plant types.

TREES ON AN ALMOST TREELESS LAND
Why aren't there many trees on grasslands? Primarily because the grassland climate is too dry for most trees to grow. And fires, whether lit by lightning, caused accidental-

• YOUR LIFE DEPENDS ON GRAMINEAE •

Whether or not you're aware of it, your life depends on grass. Just look at what you eat for breakfast. Whatever it is, it's probably made from grass. Cold cereal, oatmeal, muffins, biscuits, toast, pancakes, and even some kinds of syrup poured over the pancakes are made from the seeds and inner parts of grass. Wheat, corn, and oats come from grass. Sugar is made from sugar cane, which is a type of grass. Pancake syrup often contains syrup of corn, which is a type of grass. Even sausages, bacon, and milk come indirectly from grass. They're produced by or made from animals that eat grass and grass products.

Grasses called cereal crops—corn, wheat, rice, millet, barley, rye, and oats—are among the principle food sources for the world. The seeds of most of these grasses are easy to grow and easy to store, ensuring a good food stock year-round. Some of these cereal crops also grow in comparatively dry conditions, which has allowed humans worldwide to expand into areas too dry for growing most other foods. People in cultures who live without growing cereal crops generally have to spend much more time hunting and gathering food, and the lands they live upon support far fewer people per acre.

As you can see, foods from grass species have had a tremendous impact on the history of human civilization. And today grass still has an impact, even in the way we travel. Ethanol, a fuel made from corn—a grass— is being used to power cars!

ly, or set intentionally by people, sweep the grasslands periodically, eliminating tree growth. Grazing animals, too, can have an impact. They trample young trees, churn up soil with their hooves, and eat young tree shoots, preventing trees from becoming established. In temperate grasslands, trees such as box elder, ash, and cottonwood may grow

A solitary cottonwood tree stands in stark contrast to the grassland surrounding it.

along rivers and streams where water is plentiful, or where people have planted them. Even these few trees can be important to the animals that live nearby.

Savanna Survivors   A special type of grassland, called savanna, has quite a few trees. Up to 30 percent of the land may be covered by trees. In the temperate zone, savanna often occurs as an ecotone, a border between forest and grassland. The northern parkland of Canada is such a savanna. And in the eastern United States, oak savanna occurs in between the tallgrass prairie and the eastern deciduous forest. In Africa, South America, and Australia, tropical grasslands often take the form of savanna, with drought-resistant baobab and acacia trees scattered over their expanses.

LIFE FOR THE GRASSLAND PLANT

For a moment, be fanciful, and imagine you're a plant. How would you survive in a dry, windy, sometimes bitterly cold, sometimes swelteringly hot place where fires are common and great herds of animals want to eat you up? Obviously, plants don't consciously decide what to do. But over thousands of years, plant species have genetically evolved, and adapted to grassland conditions.

As discussed in this chapter, some grassland plants grow extensive roots, grow upward from their base, or have chemicals to deter grazers. Some make lots of seeds, seeds that survive for a long time in the soil, or seeds that stick onto animals' hides. Overall, the adaptations of grassland plants are varied and remarkable. In fact, there are so many thousands of grassland plant species—each adapted to the environment in its own unique way—that it's hard to generalize about what characteristics are best for grassland survival.

≈5≋
GRASSLAND ANIMALS

For animals, grassland life is very different from forest life. Grasslands don't provide many trees to climb on, perch in, or build nests upon. Small animals can't rely on nuts, bark, sap, or other tree products for food. And for big animals, there's almost no place to hide from predators. Still, even without the plentiful trees and shrubs of a forest, grassland animals survive. Over thousands and millions of years, they've evolved distinctive lifestyles suited to their grassland home.

GRASSLAND DINING

If you're going to live in a grassland, why not eat grass? One reason is that grass and other plants have tough cell walls that can be difficult to digest. To combat this problem, bison and pronghorns have evolved special stomachs to do the job. These animals, called ruminants, swallow grass, then digest it bit by bit, with the help of bacteria and other microorganisms contained in their stomachs. Tough wads of grass, called cud, are regurgitated, chewed again, then swallowed again. Ruminants aren't the only animals adapted to eating grass. Pocket gophers' lips close right behind their incisors, preventing soil from getting in their mouth while they're digging for, or dining on, grass roots.

Meat Eaters   Perhaps the next best thing to eating grass is to eat something that eats grass. Rodents, insects, grazing mammals, birds, and other plant eaters, all of which are plentiful on grasslands, often become meals for wolves, badgers, hawks, owls, and other predators. Among grassland predators, hunting techniques vary. Grassland birds such as hawks and eagles use their sharp eyesight to spot mice before swooping down to grasp them in their talons. Wolves hunt in packs to bring down bison, while larks snatch beakfuls of insects, right off the ground.

Water Woes   Since grasslands experience periods of dryness, many grassland creatures must make due with little water at times. Ground squirrels and kangaroo rats obtain much of their water from the seeds, fruits, stems, and leaves they eat. They also conserve water by sweating very little and keeping cool in underground burrows during the heat of the day. Additionally, their bodies conserve water by reducing the amount of water lost through urine.

MORE ON GRASSLAND LIFESTYLES

To escape cold winds, winter snows, midday heat, hungry predators, or quick-moving fires, a good place to go is underground. Just a few inches below the ground's surface it can be cool on a hot summer day, and relatively warm even while a cold winter storm rages above. During fast-moving prairie fires, little of the soil gets burned, so a burrow can be a safe refuge then, too. No wonder the burrowing lifestyle is so common in grasslands.

Many grassland animals are pros at burrow building. In one night, a pocket gopher can dig 300 feet (91 meters) of new tunnel. Unfortunately for the gophers, prairie dogs, and other prey animals, predatory badgers are good diggers, too. A badger will dig into a tunnel after a rodent, quickly widening the opening with its powerful paws.

Tunnel Towns   Prairie dogs, which aren't dogs at all, but instead a kind of ground squirrel, are among the most famous of grassland burrowers. They live in large colonies, called "prairie dog towns," that can cover many acres of land and reach to depths of 12 to 15 feet (3.6 to 4.5 meters). Belowground, their accommodations include winding passageways, grass-lined sleeping areas, chambers for food, and even "bathrooms," where droppings are deposited. Burrow entrances are built into elevated mounds, so that water does not flood passageways. Additionally, the mounds serve as lookout points for prairie dog sentries, who stand tall on their hind legs, getting a good view of the land.

Run for It   If you don't have a burrow to dive into, then run. On grasslands, where there's little cover, running is a good way to evade predators. With long legs and a super-large heart, a pronghorn can reach speeds of 60 miles per hour (97 kilometers per hour) as it runs, mouth open, gulping air. Even a jackrabbit can reach 45 miles per hour (73 kilometers per hour) at full hop. But running isn't a fool-proof way to escape because grassland predators run fast, too. Africa's cheetahs, the world's fastest land mammals, can reach speeds of 70 miles per hour (113 kilometers per hour) on short sprints. A coyote can achieve a good clip of 40 miles per hour (65 kilometers per hour). And wolves, by working in coordinated groups, like relay racers, can tire out even speedy prey.

Social Life   Herding, flocking, or banding together, grassland animals often gather in large groups. Millions of bison once gathered in herds that took more than a day to pass by a given point. In 1901 a government biologist found a virtual "rodent megalopolis," a prairie dog town 100 miles (161 kilometers) wide, 250 miles (403 kilometers) long, with over 400 million prairie dogs in residence. Even today geese, blackbirds, sparrows, and other grassland birds may travel, feed, and settle in flocks of hundreds or thousands.

Group Dynamics Why travel in a pack, band, flock, or herd? Because it's a good defense against predators in these wide-open spaces, where there is little cover. Animals in large groups can take turns keeping a lookout for predators. (Grassland predators and prey tend to have good vision, the better to keep an eye on each other!) When a predator approaches, pronghorns contract their rump muscles, raising white hairs in a powder-puff flash of alarm. Prairie dog "scouts" stand watch on their hind legs. If a predator approaches, the prairie dog whistles loudly and all the prairie dogs dive into their burrows. Scientists suspect another reason some animals may stick together is because living in large groups eliminates the need to search far and wide for mates. Whatever the reason for their gatherings, many grassland animals have evolved to live in large groups, and have developed complex social systems as a result of this lifestyle.

Birdy Behavior Grassland birds often behave quite differently from their forest cousins. More than half of all grassland birds nest on the ground. Burrowing owls even nest underground! Grassland courtship is a challenge, too. On windy grasslands, sounds such as bird song do not travel well. So some birds perch on tall grasses to give their calls, while others sing while flying—a habit uncommon in birds of other biomes. Perhaps strangest of all, grassland birds such as grouse, quail, and roadrunners, often run to escape predators, even though they can fly. On Africa's grasslands, ostriches are so adapted for running, they can no longer fly at all!

Hard Times Some grassland animals must adapt to survive bitterly cold winters. American bison grow thick, shaggy coats. Grassland rodents stock up—storing seeds and other foods in their burrows for both cold winters and droughts. And toads, prairie dogs, and gophers hibernate underground. In hibernation, their body temperature and rate of metabolism drop, enabling them to survive winter periods of cold and food scarcity.

GRASSLAND INSECTS

At times, the biggest consumer of grassland plants is not grazing bison or pronghorn, but insects. Can you imagine walking outside your house and finding yourself, and everything else, covered with grasshoppers? They crunch under your feet, they eat everything in sight, and the sound of their wings is so loud it makes a dull roar. These hordes of grasshoppers occur periodically on grasslands throughout the world. In 1870, Nebraskans reported a grasshopper swarm 30 miles (48 kilometers) wide, 100 miles (161 kilometers) long, and 1 mile (1.6 kilometers) high. The swarm took six hours to pass, and contained an estimated 124 billion grasshoppers.

Terrible Plagues *Locust* is the term scientists use for grasshoppers when they are swarming. In a normal year, grasshopper populations stay small. Disease, parasites, and predators such as birds take their toll. But in certain years, particularly after droughts, their numbers may increase while the forces that reduce their populations decrease. The locust population grows rapidly and gathers, flying in swarms so big they block out the sun for miles. These locusts eat just about every seed, leaf, and plant stalk in their path.

World of Insects Of course locust plagues are rare, occurring only infrequently. Most of the time prairie insects such as stinkbugs, ambush beetles, lady beetles, scarab beetles, dragonflies, and the hundreds of grasshopper species, carry on their lives almost unnoticed by humans. They eat plants,

Grasshoppers in a field of alfalfa might be joined by billions of others in a season when grasshoppers are swarming.

decaying matter, and other insects, and become food for a variety of creatures, including birds, snakes, and rodents. Small creatures—not just insects, but also other inverte-brates and microorganisms, play a critical role in the prairie community.

A LAND FOR WILDLIFE

It's almost hard to picture the North American grasslands that the early European settlers saw in 1600. Back then there were an estimated 50 million bison, 2 million wolves, 45

· SYMBOL OF THE PRAIRIE: THE AMERICAN BISON ·

Six feet (1.8 meters) high at the shoulder, and weighing almost a ton (0.9 metric ton), American bison are nothing less than impressive. Their bellowing call, which can be heard for miles, has been compared to the sound of distant thunder. The ground literally shakes when massive male bison engage in "headbutting" battles to establish dominance over the herd. Bison, also nicknamed "buffalo," were the dominant feature of North America's prairies until a century ago.

For thousands of years, these huge plant eaters roamed the continent, moving in herds of 50 to 200, but banding together in herds of several million at times. Moving from place to place prevented these herbivores from overgrazing, for the most part. Their ranges overlapped only slightly with pronghorns, which were more common in the dry, western prairies. Yet even where their ranges overlapped, there was little competition between them because bison ate mostly grass, while pronghorns ate primarily cacti, forbs, and shrubs.

Up to 50 million American bison covered the plains of North America when European-American settlers arrived. Today the bisons' well-worn trails and the places where they wallowed—took dust baths—can still be seen on America's prairies, even though the last large herds were slaughtered in 1882. In just 30 years, the bisons' numbers had been reduced from 50 million to about 1,000. Tiny, scattered remnant herds in Canada and in America's Yellowstone Park survived the slaughter. Today these herds are thriving on protected lands. More herds are being reintroduced to their former ranges. And many people believe that the American bison, the symbol of the prairie, may finally return to its former range. (For more on bison, see "Where the Buffalo Roam," chapter 7.)

Thick, shaggy fur helps bison endure the cold winters common on the North American prairie.

million pronghorns, and untold numbers of prairie dogs, jackrabbits, badgers, deer, elk, eagles, foxes, skunks, shrews, prairie chickens, snakes, larks, and other creatures. Today, these creatures survive in limited numbers, in certain areas. About 1,200 wolves live in the lower 48 states, and 135,000 bison live in Canada and the United States. But even by observing these animals in limited numbers, you can begin to appreciate the wonderful ways they have adapted to the very special demands of grassland life.

✵6✵
GRASSLAND
COMMUNITIES

Be warned. If you peek into a prairie dog hole, you might find more than you expected. Snakes, weasels, black-footed ferrets, burrowing owls, and toads have all been known to take up residence in abandoned prairie dog burrows. Not only do prairie dog burrows provide shelter for other creatures, but by building them, prairie dogs help mix and aerate the soil, increasing its fertility. By excavating dirt, and clipping the grass near their burrows, prairie dogs create bare spots where certain plants thrive and others do not. These spots also attract bison, which find them perfect for vigorous, back-scratching, body-rolling, dust baths that clean their shaggy coats of parasites.

Like the prairie dog, each animal, plant, fungus, and bacterium affects the lives of other organisms within its biological community. Grasslands, and all biomes for that matter, are made up of such connections, which link all the inhabitants of a natural community.

GO WITH THE FLOW

Energy flow links together the animals and plants in a natural community. In a grassland, energy in the form of sunlight is used by grass to make sugars, which are stored as starch in its leaves, roots, shoots, and seeds. When that grass is eaten by a grasshopper, some, but not all, of the energy in the leaves becomes part of the grasshopper. Part of that energy is lost in the process, as it is at every stage when

By living in large groups, prairie dogs can help one another keep watch for the many predators that hunt them.

energy is transferred from one organism to another. When a thirteen-lined ground squirrel eats the grasshopper, and a wolf eats the thirteen-lined ground squirrel, part of the energy from each organism is transferred to the next. When the wolf dies, scavengers such as turkey vultures eat its body, and a portion of that energy becomes part of them. Finally, decomposers—worms, bacteria, fungi, and small insects—finish up the job, eating the rest. The leftovers and by-products of their meals then become part of the soil. A simple diagram of energy links such as the ones described above is called a food chain. Several food chains, linked together, create a food web—a diagram ecologists use to show the energy relationships between many organisms in a community.

MEASURES OF LIFE

It's obvious when you look at a grassland that there's less "stuff" growing on it than grows in most forests. To measure such a difference, biologists measure plant biomass—the weight of the roots, shoots, leaves, and other plant material that exists in a certain area. Grasslands have less plant biomass than temperate deciduous forests. But it's not just how much plant biomass is in an area, but how it's distributed that makes each biome unique. In an oak forest, less than 10 percent of the plant biomass is underground. Yet in a grassland, the bulk of plant matter—70 percent of it on average—is belowground. These underground tissues gather water, store food, and help plants survive and regrow after fire or grazing.

Diversity Compared to other biomes, grasslands have a moderate number of animal and plant species—a moderate species diversity. In general, grasslands contain few species that are endemic—unique to the area. Deserts, and temperate deciduous forests, for instance, tend to have many more species that live only in those biomes. There are, however, exceptions to the rule. Certain spots such as untouched tallgrass prairie do support many unique species. And the wetter the grassland, the more species it contains.

Population In grasslands, animal and plant populations can fluctuate because of climatic factors. In dry years, for

---

• TELLING TEMPERATURE BY CRICKET •

Animals and plants in the prairie community depend on weather. For instance, in warm weather, crickets chirp more often than in cold weather. This phenomenon is so predictable that you can count how many times a cricket (not a grasshopper) chirps in a 15-second period. Then add 40 to that number, and the sum should be the temperature, roughly, in Fahrenheit degrees.

instance, prickly pear cacti become common in grassland on the Great Plains, while in wet years they practically disappear from the landscape. Grasshoppers increase in dry years. And populations of voles, jackrabbits, deer mice, birds, and other grassland animals have also been known to fluctuate widely because of drought and drought-related factors.

PREDATORS, PREY, AND POISON

What is a prairie without wolves, coyotes, golden eagles, and black-footed ferrets? Some people would say it's not truly prairie. Biologically, predators are important. They play a role in keeping down the number of prey animals. Many predators cull easy-to-catch, weak, or sick animals from a population, thereby keeping a prey population healthy by weeding out ill-adapted animals. Obviously, predators are an important part of a natural community. But that is little comfort to ranchers and farmers whose chickens, goats, sheep, pigs, or cattle are occasionally killed by predators.

Increased Conflict Conflicts between predators and people have been going on for years. But in the 1800s, as European-American settlers moved farther out onto the prairies, conflicts with wolves, coyotes, and eagles intensified. North America's prairies became the site of one of the most extensive and bloodiest predator persecution programs in history. Coyotes, wolves, and eagles were shot, trapped, and poisoned by the thousands. State and local governments paid bounties to professional and amateur hunters for each predator killed. Wolves were exterminated from most of their former prairie range, dropping from a population of 2 million to just 1,200 in the lower 48 states.

Part of the tragedy of the predator poisoning programs is that they unintentionally killed many nontarget animals, which ate the poisoned bait or ate carcasses of poisoned animals. The widespread use of poisons by sheep ranchers continued up to the 1970s. Today predators such as wolves, eagles, and bears are partially protected by law in parts of their range. Coyotes, despite people's attempts to kill them off, seem to be increasing in number and expanding their range much farther into the eastern United States than ever before. But predator control programs on a smaller scale still continue, and are a subject of controversy in some parts of the country.

Black-footed Ferret   One predator, the black-footed ferret, has become an endangered species not because of direct persecution, but because of the persecution of its prey: the prairie dog. Seen as an agricultural pest, prairie dogs have been killed off by the millions over the last century. Now these rodents, once abundant, are scarce, even endangered in some states. Their primary food source gone, black-footed ferrets have become endangered. Today, efforts to breed black-footed ferrets in captivity may help this species avoid extinction. But prairie dog persecution still continues. So even if the black-footed ferrets recover, they could only be reintroduced into limited areas, because prairie dogs are plentiful on just 2 percent of their former range.

PRAIRIE FIRE: THE GOOD, THE BAD, AND THE BURNED

A grassland fire can be fearsome to behold. Fanned by strong prairie winds, flames can leap 40 feet (12 meters) high, raising temperatures 3 feet (0.9 meter) aboveground to a scorching 400°F (204°C). As the grass burns, bison stampede, birds fly from their flaming nests, pronghorns race away, and gophers dive into their burrows, where the soil remains tolerably cool.

A Natural Process   Fire is a natural part of grassland life. Lightning storms spark the dry grass, starting fires. These

Working with black-footed ferrets in captivity, scientists are struggling to keep this species alive.

lightning-caused fires naturally occur about every 3 to 30 years. For thousands of years, humans have also set fires intentionally to attract game to the new grass that grows after a fire has passed through an area.

Regrowth and Renewal   In many ways, fire is good for grassland. Prairie fires are hot but move quickly, driven by the wind. As a result, they do little damage to the soil and underground roots. From roots and seeds held in the soil, plants can quickly regrow on the burned soil. And the fire helps increase plant growth overall by ridding the ground of old stalks, leaving fresh black ash, an ideal fertilizer. All this helps certain plants to grow. In parts of the tallgrass prairie, where trees tend to take over the prairie lands, fires can help eliminate shrubs and saplings, allowing prairie grasses and forbs to thrive. In prairie preserves around North America, managers periodically set controlled fires to mimic natural prairie conditions.

PRAIRIE SUCCESSION

Sometimes bare spots—areas without any plants—form in a grassland. These spots may occur where bison have wallowed, cattle have overgrazed, or a particularly hot fire has burned. But these bare spots don't last for long. Aggressive pioneer plants soon take hold. Many pioneer plants are annuals, which sprout from seeds blown in on the wind, or seeds long lying dormant in the soil.

March of Life   Pioneer plants hold the soil in place and create conditions that make it easier for other kinds of grasses and forbs to grow. Over the years, the grassland's appearance changes, as different species dominate the scene. This process of change is called succession. How well the grassland regrows on a bare spot depends on many different factors, including soil health, weather, how big the spot is, and the proximity of seed sources—other grassland patches.

TAKE A HIKE IN GRASSLAND

As in any other biome, you should dress for the weather in a grassland. In summer be sure to bring a sun hat and plenty of water, so you won't get sunstroke or dehydrated. Know where you're going, tell someone of your plans, bring a map, and carry enough food to keep your energy level high.

Here are just a few of the things you can look for, smell for, and listen for on a grassland hike:

• Mound entrances to prairie dog burrows;
• The whistle of a prairie dog;

- The rattle of a prairie rattlesnake;
- A golden eagle soaring overhead;
- The drumming sound of a prairie chicken calling for a mate;
- A flight of ducks or geese heading for a prairie pothole;
- Fragrant mint leaves;
- Insects swimming in the tiny puddles held between the cupplant's leaves;
- The bones of ancient bison;
- Cottonwood trees along a grassland stream;
- A tiger beetle in search of prey;
- Butterflies landing on purple bee balm blooms;
- Raccoon pawprints near a stream;
- The yellow flowers of a prickly pear cactus;
- Prickly seeds that can latch onto an animal's fur . . . or you!

ECOTONES: THE IN-BETWEEN LANDS

Where does grassland end and another biome begin? The borders of North America's grasslands are abrupt in some places. Within a few hundred yards, a forest and its plants can end and a grassland begin. In other places, a gentler transition occurs, creating an ecotone, an area where the plants and animals of two biomes mingle. In Canada, grassland and boreal forest mingle in an ecotone called northern aspen parkland. There the ground is mostly covered by grass, but aspen and boreal conifers grow scattered across the land. Between the temperate deciduous forest and prairie lies another ecotone, the eastern oak savanna. It has many of the grass species characteristic of prairie, but has trees of the eastern deciduous forest as well.

PRAIRIE POTHOLES

Flying over the farmlands of North Dakota, Manitoba, and other northern prairie lands, you can look down on a landscape more full of holes than Swiss cheese. These thousands of holes—actually water-filled depressions—are special wetlands called prairie potholes. Created by glaciers as they receded, these potholes range from a fifth of an acre (less than a tenth of a hectare) to 25 acres (10 hectacres) in size. There were once so many of these potholes that European-American settlers wrote of ice-skating in winter from farm to farm! In the last century, however, farmers have drained many of these wetlands to create farmable soil.

For the Birds Potholes play an important role in the prairie habitat. They hold rainwater and floodwater and then slowly release it, helping to prevent floods and erosion. They're home to aquatic animals and plants, and are a water source for wild animals nearby. Over half of North America's waterfowl use these small wetlands as a nesting site, or a stopover site for resting and feeding during their migration. Many conservationists, concerned about the rapid loss of these small wetlands, are working to strengthen Federal legislation that gives farmers incentives to preserve these areas.

PEOPLE AND THE GRASSLAND

For thousands of years, Native Americans lived primarily on prairie edges, harvesting forest products, planting crops in river floodplains, but only periodically venturing out on the prairie to hunt bison. For most of the year the prairie belonged to the bison, the wolf, the prairie dog, the wind. But then things changed dramatically. Over the last 500 years, by horse, by plow, and by tractor, North Americans have made grassland their domain. Major cities such as Chicago and Los Angeles have been built on former grasslands. And today millions of people's food supply depends upon prairie farms and ranches.

RECENT HISTORY OF CHANGE

When Spanish explorers came to North America in the 1500s, life for many of North America's grassland dwellers changed. Not just because the Spanish and European-Americans took over land, but also because they brought horses. Before horses came along, how far and fast Native Americans could travel depended on how much they and their dogs could carry or pull in sleds. But once horses became widespread through trade, Native Americans could move far and fast, and carry all their belongings, and utilize the prairies as never before. As a result, when European-Americans moved farther into the forested country, some Native American tribes were able to move farther out on the prairies, developing a more nomadic life, following the bison herds, and relying almost exclusively on them for food.

End of an Era   In the late 1800s, this grassland way of life was annihilated. Native Americans were systematically persecuted, rounded up, and placed on reservations. The bison they depended upon were slaughtered, hundreds at a time, by European-American hunters who skinned them, leaving their meat to rot. This widespread slaughter was designed to clear the prairies for cattle. It also forced Native Americans to give up bison hunting and move to Indian reservations where they would be provided with government beef. The lives of people in North America's grassland would never be the same.

THE FARMING OF THE PRAIRIES

Like so many humans before them, most early European-American settlers clung to forest edges, preferring to clear forest for farmland instead of planting out on the prairie. After all, the forest was familiar, and wood and game were readily available within it. But in the late 1800s, European-Americans came west to the prairie in droves, attracted by government incentives and the promises of land speculators. Soon, the forest and forest edges were settled. And people had to move farther out into the prairie.

Sodbusters   To establish their prairie farms, settlers had to sodbust—break up the tough, root-bound prairie sod. This was tedious, awkward, backbreaking work, requiring several teams of oxen just to pull one plow. In 1833, prairie agriculture was revolutionized by the invention of the steel plow, which was light, strong, slick, and easier to use than the old iron plows. Within a few years, a blacksmith named John Deere began producing steel plows for widespread

Wheat and other crops grown on rich prairie soils provide food for much of North America.

use, and within a few decades, the prairie was largely plowed under. The tallgrass prairie became the cornbelt—the corn-growing region of today. The mixed-grass prairie became the breadbasket, the wheat-growing region. And farther west, with the help of railways, short-grass prairies and desert grassland became cattle range.

ENVIRONMENTAL CHALLENGES
FOR THE FUTURE

Today, despite the changes that have occurred in the last 500 years, North America's grasslands still hold sights of tremendous beauty. There are Wyoming ranges where pronghorns roam, North Dakota wetlands where geese gather and frogs call, and Indiana cornfields where thousands of sandhill cranes stop over to feed and rest on their migration south. People who want to preserve these remaining wildlife spectacles, and ensure healthy prairie soils, are concerned about the following threats to the prairie's future:

Farming Conversion of prairie to cropland is the number one cause of grassland destruction; it continues to be a problem today. Loss of topsoil also threatens the survival of grassland farms that already exist, pushing farmers to plant crops on marginal lands such as very wet and very dry soils.

Overgrazing Cattle, sheep, and goats, if grazed too long in an area, damage grassland plants and soil, churn up dirt with their hooves, and cause erosion. These animals also pollute streams with fecal contaminants.

Development As urban and suburban areas expand, the need for space for homes, roads, shopping malls, and other human development is increasingly a threat to grasslands, particularly in the heavily populated tallgrass prairie region.

Water Overuse Water is a scarce commodity on most prairies. Many of the towns, cities, and farms of the Great Plains rely on water pumped from deep underground, where it lies in the Ogallala Aquifer, a layer of porous rock. This water is replenished as rainwater trickles through the ground to recharge the aquifer. Today the Ogallala Aquifer is being used up too quickly and is expected to be almost depleted within the next century.

Human Population Growth As human population increases worldwide, the need to live on, farm, or graze animals on grasslands increases. This growth, overall, accelerates grassland destruction in many ways.

Global Climate Change Airborne pollutants from industry, cars, burning forests, and other sources are causing

· GRASSLANDS AND STARVING AFRICA ·

You see them on television, in newspapers, in magazines: the faces of thousands of people starving to death in Africa. What does their plight have to do with grasslands? A lot. Sometimes these people's starvation is caused by wars and political problems in their countries. But very often it has to do with drought, a natural feature of grasslands.

During rainy years, people tend to forget about the droughts that can leave grassland parched for years. When rain is plentiful, people bear more children, plant more crops, and increase the size of their livestock herds. People and livestock spread out even onto marginal land. Then, when the next drought occurs, crops fail. Plants that livestock depend on die. And people starve. The remaining livestock overgraze bushes, trees, and whatever grass is left. People cut down the last trees for firewood. Soil blows away. Even worse, all these activities damage the land to such an extent that it often cannot recover when rain does return.

This cycle of destruction leads to desertification, the process by which fertile grassland, forest, or semi-arid desert turns into arid, virtually lifeless, desert. Desertification is a problem in at least 100 countries worldwide. Fifteen million acres (6 million hectares) of land become lifeless desert each year. The Sahara Desert, once a grassland itself, is increasing in size. Desertification has a terrible human toll, leaving people homeless, without land for growing crops, leading to further famine.

Scientists disagree over whether people or climate is the main cause of current desertification. Throughout the history of the earth, grasslands have naturally expanded, contracted, and shifted position as the earth's climate changed. However, many scientists feel that even if climate change is the underlying cause, people's activities are certainly accelerating the process in many parts of the world. Climate changes causing desertification may also be connected to global warming, the predicted change in the world's climate as a result of air pollution released by cars, factories, volcanoes, and other pollution sources.

changes in the earth's climate. This is sometimes called global warming. The effect of global climate change on grasslands is uncertain, but some scientists predict the shifting of weather patterns could, in the future, change areas that are currently grassland to desert.

Mining, Oil and Gas Drilling, and Toxic Waste   Parts of the prairie region lie atop oil, gas, and mineral deposits that are being harvested, causing pollution. Sparsely populated prairie regions are increasingly being used as dump sites for toxic waste, and for nuclear waste storage.

Introduction of Exotic Species   In many grasslands, non-native plants, called exotics, have taken hold. These plants, such as bromegrass, Kentucky bluegrass, blindweed, and leafy spurge, quickly colonize the soil, making it difficult for native prairie plants to become established.

Of course, often it's not one, but a combination of the above factors that leads to the destruction of a prairie.

HOME ON THE RANGE:
GRASSLAND CONSERVATION

From the sand hills of Nebraska to the prairie potholes of South Dakota to the tallgrass prairie remnants in Illinois, a movement to save the remaining North American grasslands is taking root, and flourishing. Here are just a few of the things being done to save and restore prairie:

• In 1990 the Nature Conservancy purchased a 30,000 acre (12,000 hectare) ranch in northeastern Oklahoma's Osage Hills in order to establish a tallgrass prairie preserve. Many other prairie preserves are popping up all over the United States.
• Canada is creating a 350-square-mile (906 square kilome-

ter) Grasslands National Park in southwest Saskatchewan.

- Elementary school students all over the prairie are reseeding parts of the areas surrounding their schools with prairie plants. These areas serve as wildlife habitats and natural outdoor biological laboratories teachers can use for their lessons.
- In Texas, citizen groups are asking highway departments to plant native wildflowers such as prairie plants along the sides of highways. These native plants provide food for butterflies, and are an enjoyable spectacle for drivers. They also save the state money since native plants require less mowing and other maintenance than traditional grass lawn.
- Environmental activists nationwide are working to get stronger laws passed to preserve prairie potholes, a critical habitat for migratory birds.
- Farmers are learning soil conservation techniques that lead to healthier soil and better crop yields.
- Biologists have reintroduced tule elk and pronghorn to California's central valley grassland. Some day the California condor, which once soared over these lands, may be returned as well.

Where the Buffalo Roam   For many people, part of restoring the prairie is restoring its bison. And bison are on the comeback trail. In Yellowstone National Park, the bison population has tripled in the last 20 years, and is now spilling out of the park. People are reintroducing bison to prairie preserves and Indian reservations. Ranchers are selling their cattle and raising bison for beef instead. And wolves are being released in Yellowstone National Park, where they once were common, but had since died out.

The Buffalo Commons   Two college professors, Frank and Deborah Popper, have proposed a 139,000-square-mile

(360,000-square-kilometer) "Buffalo Commons," a preserve where reintroduced bison would roam free. The bison would roam in prairie states such as Nebraska, Montana, Oklahoma, and the Dakotas, where many counties are losing human population at a rapid rate, as farms and ranches fail, and people move to other parts of the country. From their studies of prairie history, the Poppers have come to believe many of these areas were settled and farmed when weather was unusually good, and that in the long run these places are too drought- and erosion-prone for conventional agriculture. They believe that these sparsely populated areas could be returned to the bison, to become a grand American wilderness.

A Future for the North American Grasslands   Certainly, the Poppers' dream of a Buffalo Commons is ambitious. But so is the work of preserving the remaining prairie and ensuring a good future for prairie soils, farms, and ranches. For some very endangered grasslands, such as tallgrass prairie, the future may lie only in restoration of small patches; it's probably not feasible for this type of grassland to blanket the large regions it once did. But for other grasslands, there is much more land that can be conserved, restored, and protected. Thousands of people who love the prairie are hard at work on these kinds of conservation projects and they could use your help. You never know what can be accomplished with small seeds and big dreams.

RESOURCES AND WHAT
YOU CAN DO TO HELP

Here's what you can do to help ensure that grasslands are conserved:

• Learn more by reading books and watching videos and television programs about the grassland. Check your local library, bookstore, and video store for resources. Here are just a few of the books available for further reading:

Grasslands by Lauren Brown (The Audubon Society Nature Guides Series) (Knopf, 1985).

Save Our Prairies and Grasslands by Ron Hirschi (Audubon One Earth Series) (Doubleday, 1994).

A Sea of Grass: The Tallgrass Prairie by David Dvorak, Jr. (Macmillan, 1994).

What Do We Know About Grasslands? by Brian Knapp (Caring for Environments Series) (Peter Bedrick, 1992).

Where the Buffalo Roam by Anne Mathews (Grove Weidenfeld, 1992).

•For more information on grassland and grassland-related issues, write or call the following organizations:

National Wildflower Research Center
2600 FM 973 North
Austin, TX 78725-4201
Phone 1-512-929-3600

The Nature Conservancy
1815 North Lynn Street
Arlington, VA 22209
Phone 1-703-841-5300

If you like the job these organizations are doing, consider becoming a member. Also, if you live in a grassland region, contact your state chapter of the Nature Conservancy to see if they have grassland projects underway in your area. You may be able to get involved in the hands-on planting, weeding, seed-gathering, and overall maintenance of a real grassland patch.

• Visit a museum, national park, national monument, or botanical garden that has grassland features or displays. The following national parks, monuments, and wildlife refuges contain grassland:

United States
Badlands National Park, Interior, SD
Big Bend National Park, Big Bend National Park, TX
Carlsbad Caverns National Park, Carlsbad, NM
Charles M. Russell National Wildlife Range, Lewistown, MT
Crescent Lake National Wildlife Refuge, Ellsworth, NE
Kern National Wildlife Refuge, Delano, CA
National Bison Range, Moiese, MT
National Elk Refuge, Jackson, WY
Theodore Roosevelt National Park, Medora, ND
Turnbull National Wildlife Refuge, Cheney, WA
Valentine National Wildlife Refuge, Valentine, NE
Wichita Mountains Wildlife Refuge, Indiahoma, OK
Yellowstone National Park, Yellowstone National Park, WY

Canada
Elk Island National Park, Edmonton, Alberta
Grasslands National Park, Val Marie, Saskatchewan
Prince Albert National Park, Prince Albert, Saskatchewan
Riding Mountain National Park, Brandon, Manitoba
Waterton Lakes National Park, Waterton Park, Alberta

• If you live in a grassland region, consider planting an area of prairie forbs and grasses. You might talk with teachers and school administrators about doing this as a school project, to create habitat for wildlife and also an outdoor laboratory where teachers can conduct lessons. For information on planting a prairie, contact the National Wildflower Research Center, whose address is in a previous entry.

• Educate others about grassland. Put on a skit at school, construct a display for the hallway or local mall to raise awareness of grassland issues.

• To find out how you can help promote better farming practices and soil conservation in general, contact the Soil Conservation Service in your area, or:

United States Department of Agriculture
Soil Conservation Service
Room 0054 South
Washington, DC 20250
Phone 1-202-720-5157

• Write letters to state and national government officials, telling them you feel grassland conservation is important.

• Conserve water by installing water-saving devices, turning off the tap while brushing your teeth, taking shorter showers, running only full loads of laundry, and so on. Water lawns in the cool of the morning or evening, when less water will evaporate into the air. Even better, encourage your family and friends to landscape with drought-resistant, native plants instead of grasses that require a lot of watering.

GLOSSARY

biome   an area that has a certain kind of climate and a certain kind of community of plants and animals

desertification   the process by which productive land that supports life is turned into lifeless desert

drought   a long period without precipitation

dust bowl   a region that suffers from dust storms caused by a long drought. This term was coined in 1936 to describe the western edge of North America's Great Plains, which suffered these conditions during the droughts of the 1930s.

ecotone   a border between two biomes, where the plants and animals of those biomes mingle

exotic species   species that are not native to a certain area

food chain   a simplified diagram showing the transfer of energy from the sun to a plant, from that plant to a plant eater, and from the plant eater to a meat eater, and so on

food web   a diagram that shows energy flow in a community by showing how the food chains in that community are linked

forb   a non-woody plant other than a grass

grass   a plant that is a member of the family Gramineae, particularly those kinds eaten by grazing animals. Grasses generally have jointed stems, a meristem at their base, long slender leaves that wrap around the stem, and inconspicuous flowers.

locust   a grasshopper that is in its migratory phase, when it gathers with other grasshoppers in large swarms

meristem   a plant's cells and tissues that are capable of growth by cell division

mixed-grass prairie   grassland with grass of medium height, found on the central plains of North America

organic matter   the remains of once-living organisms

prairie   a term used for some grasslands in North America

prairie pothole   a relatively small freshwater wetland created by the action of glaciers on prairie lands

predator   an animal that catches and eats other animals

ruminant   an animal that has a many-chambered stomach and chews cud, meaning it chews, swallows, coughs up, and then rechews tough-to-digest grasses

savanna   a tropical grassland that has widely scattered trees and plants that are resistant to drought

short-grass prairie   the grassland, featuring short, drought-resistant grasses, that grows on the western portion of North America's Great Plains

sod   the dense, thick prairie surface, made up of soil held together by intertwined plant roots and runners

tallgrass prairie   the grassland, featuring tall grasses, that grows on the eastern edge of North America's Great Plains

temperate grasslands   grasslands that occur in the temperate region, which is between the Tropic of Cancer and the Arctic Circle in the Northern Hemisphere, and between the Tropic of Capricorn and the Antarctic Circle in the Southern Hemisphere

topsoil   soil on the ground's surface

tropical grasslands   grasslands that occur in the tropics: the region stretching from the Tropic of Capricorn to the Tropic of Cancer

INDEX